As I read the poems in Fred Rosenblum's *Tramping Solo*, I found myself as one of the *"Beavers"* who had grown up with TV westerns and army life (be it under Sgts. Bilko or Saunders), looking at a life's journey that might have been mine. In poem after poem he takes us to places most of us will never have the need to go, whether it is as a deckhand on an Alaskan salmon seiner, or as a jack-of-all-trades...master of none in a sawmill. Being a freight riding Jason on a Santa Fe Argo searching for his own golden fleecing. As always, Mr. Rosenblum is a master of craft, building his poems with an eccentric yet exquisite vocabulary and intense imagery. In "Stargazing" he has crafted what I consider to be one of the most amazing images ever created. I will leave it to you to discover this line on your own. In his bittersweet finale, "Still Smoldering After All These Years," he describes his and likely many veteran's memories of combat that can be rekindled by seemingly innocuous fireworks. So let's climb into Fred's treehouse that overlooks the Russian cemetery and take a look *at all of those people* that he met and worked with in those years of personal discovery.
— Tim Calaway , author of *The Green of Scullymist*

Reminiscent and transcendent of Jack London, these vivid poems are still-burning coals drawn from a buried past, exuding the language, fear, regret, and wounded hope of the 1970s. The vignettes lived in these pages span the momentous to the mundane, but Fred Rosenblum's voice is always loud and clear.
— Christopher Fields, editor, *Neologism Poetry Journal Massachusetts*

Fred Rosenblum, military nom de guerre Spunky, is not going to let us off easy. He's the anti-romantic — a blue-collar poet and bus driver's son with an affinity for the Beats' drug-induced poetic style. He saw combat in Vietnam, returned home and took to the road, destined for Alaska and positions as a deckhand on a commercial fishing boat, and a day laborer at the Sitka Pulp Mill — jobs that would sustain him when he wasn't stoned out of his mind. Fred's Alaska is not the nature writer's Alaska, forcing us to look at how things were in this country during the 60's and 70's. It's a road trip worth taking but don't expect to be comforted — do expect to be unable to put this book down.
— Tom Sexton, former Poet Laureate of Alaska whose latest collection is entitled *Cummiskey Alley*

Tramping Solo tells the story of a war vet being released from the military in the insane year of 1969, when popular culture everywhere was against the military. Interestingly, Fred Rosenblum is able to manage these experiences without attempting to moralize or teach. As a writer, he prefers to simply paint a picture and allow the reader to feel the experience of one man through language. His images present strongly without the use of common jargon, i.e. 'flashbacks' and 'ptsd': *silver satanic angels with their ravaging Phantom strikes, to this very day still strafe me.* Events are presented clearly and without comment or prejudice: *The city snarled and bared its fangs when I came out into the street with my honorable discharge and my purple fucking heart — to be wrestled to the ground on the San Diego downtown sidewalk concrete pavement ...* or *encrypted words/mantras seeping out/from the soft sponge of earth* – The story follows the vet through his travels along the Pacific Coast. The voice of the poet comes through clearly with specifically chosen imagery denoting a sense of place: *a placid evening's radiant veil of embers appearing to respire on the lighted bluffs above Monterey Bay.* We follow the vet through several years of physical duress and psychic turmoil: *Unable to acquire a prosthetic psyche in Seventy-two, my pathetic character came unglued and I ramped-up my tolerance for goofballs and booze.* Nature provides the release for both vet and reader during important transitions: *the mating call of a horned owl growling at silhouettes framed on the face of a vanishing moon ...*

— r. soos, editor, *Cholla Needles*

> *"...and the Kerouac/within me cried*
> *'cuz me had a certain/ bonhomie with alcoholic poets,*
> *vogues and bums...*

says the speaker of one of Fred Rosenblum's collected poems from *Tramping Solo*. And that bonhomie suffuses this Howl of a collection, often revealing itself in cascading verses you could imagine rolling off of Kerouac's own typewriter on an endless spool of teletype paper — verses that propel themselves into the sky like a rocket, then explode with a "Pop" and everyone says "Aww!" But, whereas the now-"Dead Beats" crossed and re-crossed this Groaning Continent with their buddies in old jalopies to a soundtrack of bebop and hot jazz, the speaker of Rosenblum's poems — not a Beat, but a "beat-up bum" — hitchhikes pretty much alone, and cops rides on boxcars from San Diego to Alaska and back — and back again — finding work in paper mills and net-fishing scows, all to the accompanying racket of: **...the screeching din of herring gulls...the defrosted whimpering/ of coyote cries...the howling of wind shears**

Rosenblum's speaker **wasn't crazy**, nor was he **queer for Canada** in 1968 during what the Vietnamese called **The American War**. No. Seduced to enlist by militaristic, jingoistic films laced with **every cliché known to man** that he'd been hooked on as a kid, his ...**nom de guerre/would be Spunky, an adrenaline junkie.**

But, honorably discharged from the Marines after a PTSD-inducing stretch of action in Southeast Asia, he finds himself **rolling stale tobacco in a 1970s San Diego lockup, plumbing slumber's darkness/ bereft of those iconic days/gathering wool in Mayfield ABC USA.**

So, **pissed at the world/for all the obvious reasons/and suffering ... the very hairy swings/of hardcore ennui**, he took to the hobo road — hungering, like the Beat poets of an earlier Post-war generation **for the spiritual richness/basic in bold,/wander lusting**

drifters. The reader of the red hot shell-casings of poetry collected in *Tramping Solo* comes to understand Rosenblum's speaker tramped unaccompanied deliberately, in white-knuckle terror of allowing the Mr. Hyde side of his PTSD-trashed psyche to rage, thus ***ruining it for everybody***. And it is the reader's great good fortune to find in the lovely final stanzas of this collection that the ***wander lusting drifter*** may just possibly have sated his — and the reader's — hunger for that elusive ***spiritual richness***.

— William Damkoehler, Actor/Playwright

Also by Fred Rosenblum

Hollow Tin Jingles

Vietnumb

Playing Chicken with an Iron Horse

Tramping Solo

Fred Rosenblum

Fomite
Burlington, Vermont

Copyright © Fred Rosenblum 2021
All rights reserved. No part of this book may be reproduced in any form or by any means without the prior written consent, except in the case of brief quotations used in reviews and certain other noncommercial uses permitted by copyright law.

Cover images
Wooden Wall: Maarten Deckers on Unsplash
Old Worn-out Boots: FreeImages.com/Renaude Hatsedakis

ISBN-13: 978-1-953236-20-3
Library of Congress Control Number: 2021934540
Fomite
58 Peru Street
Burlington, VT 05401

In Memory of
Gerald Robert Rosenblum
1943 - 2006

Acknowledgments

Some of the poems in this collection were initially published by the following:

Cholla Needles, *Cirque Magazine*, *Empty Sink*, *San Diego Reader*, and *Southeast Missouri State University Press*

Contents

Concerning what follows:

Inspired by a Former Foe	1
Fragmentations	9
The Blue Cue	11
Leaving It to the "Beavers" of America	14
Beyond the Summer of Bummers and Love	18
Home Sweet Hypocrisy	20
The City Snarled	21
Man in the Window (Hillcrest 1969) for "The Fin"	22
Bouncing Around	25
Between the Castle and Cannery Row	27
Many Rivers to Remind Me	30
Enamored of the Art	33
Sitka	35
Jamming With Dead Russians	36
In Town They Called Our Craft a Creek-Robbing Scow	37
Martha	39
Mending Seine	41
Pride of the Sound	46
Family Doctor	49
Black's Beach, Pacific Ocean	51
Bakersfield to Fresno	53
The Mill	54
Hot Springs	56
On the Bum in '72	58
Anticipating a Job in the Valley	61
Under a Bridge in the Pouring Rain	64
High Desert	66
Stargazing	68

Sundown Jungle Texarkana	71
Tribute to the Dead Beats	74
Wood Smoke Tracking the Tanana	76
Really Big Fucking Hands and Feet	77
Hunting Trip	79
In the Zen of the River	80
Still Smoldering After All These Years	83
About the Author	86

Concerning what follows:

The poems presented herein track a period of homelessness and social withdrawal I experienced following my release from the Marine Corps in 1969. They are a portrait of a Vietnam veteran who, part of a diaspora of weary warriors, went north to Alaska in the 70's hoping to find work in logging camps, on commercial fishing boats, in the slime lines of the seasonal canneries, or most lucratively, fighting fires in the state's interior summer tinderbox. Initially though, some of us moved north to find ourselves jobless and camping out in the rainforests, as I did, while others holed-up in remote cabins and sadly ended their suffering with . . . use your imagination.

I had an advantage back then over a lot of the others: a bindlestiff at heart, having aspired to the tramp life as a teen, I'd studied the culture in depth. Hitchhiking, hopping freight trains, bumming around was entirely voluntary for me. Apart from the half year detour east in '72, and 3 months spent in Thailand, I'd yo-yo up and down the Pacific Coast from California to Alaska three times between the spring of 1970 and the summer of 1973 —rife with a strong sense for wayfaring and wilderness thrills, while thwarted by a rucksack full of post-traumatic stress attached to me like a barnacle feeding on the hull of my ship-wrecked soul.

For the most part, these poems, from a very condensed space in time, present the altered state of my helter-skelter mind — tramping solo in that period of jazz cigarettes and psychedelia.. Yet, after that brief, arduous period of mental anguish and substance abuse, my journey took a positive turn when I met another lonesome traveler in Sitka, Alaska and who has long since become my wife.

Inspired by a Former Foe

"Only those who never fought like to argue who won or lost"
— Bao Ninh, author of *The Sorrow of War*

A disturbed young man,
I hadn't yet begun
to realize what I'd
been through when I
hastened-off to Sitka
in the spring of 1970,
attempting to rid myself
of everything I knew
would malign me.
Twenty-five hundred miles
north I'd thumb and
ferry, yet, amid that
which I'd dreamt —
a Londonesque sketch
of adventure, I'd verily
come face to face
with those age old,
intrusive, hairy
mementos of human
savagery, whereupon,
I'd fire-up a bowl
of medicine, gradually
become receptive to
the whispering prompts
blowing-in off the
vestiges of winter —

slight arctic breezes
that carried on them
the chants of the Tlingit
spirits who'd set a pace
for me on my upstream
treks into the ancestral
heartbeat of Southeast
Alaska, and where the
cyclical nature of
magnificent extremes
spoke totemic in vernal
speak — nonstop vociferations
of snowmelt and spills, mists
that filled the Tongass air
in the panhandle wilds
of the Last Frontier.

In no way
was any of this
remotely comparable, but
rather, in direct contrast
to the heft of the
rucksack muling I'd
previously endured
just two years prior in Southeast Asia —
nothing like the humidity
and the violent risks
to life and loss of limb
out on the tropical
mountainside spines

skirting the scarred,
undulating demarcations
of Laos and Vietnam.

We had our crosses to bear,
plights despised, in the denizen's
squint of hard-pressed eyes
from whence, those myriad
conical wicker brims
hid an odium of stares. Yes,
our gallantry and sacrifice
went unrequited —
they didn't fucking want
us there, but regardless,
we trudged on, fatigued as
Jesus ascending Golgotha,
staggering columns of
onward Christians,
soldiering into the
hill tribe colonies — hooches
contiguous to a murmuring
stream — serene and stoic
on stilts, while we,
profane, leather-necking
gyrene interlopers pushed on —
on through their chickens
and pigs — on and into the
step-ever-so-lightly trails
that led to the palpable,
yet subtle spleen
of that late afternoon
calm before contact.

Into the piss-yourself
apprehension of the firefight
rainforest mist, after which,
a tally of the
ready-for-dust-off dead
and wounded was taken.
The sweltering, sulfuric air
held the steamy metallic stench
of blood and evacuation,
married to the jungle's rotted
respirations of floral decay.

Before the sun
would abandon us, we'd
dig into the red earth clay
— lay there in the
late night laterite, ponchos
propped in such a way
so as to collect the
sweet pools of rainwater
and protect most of
the killing tools we'd carry
into the morrow. Onto
and off of those
gun trucks — small arms,
thumpers and hogs — always
wary of the dreaded,
deleterious rust effect
of the monsoon's,
miserable gusty lungs
— coughing and wheezing,
blustering through

the 17th parallel's jungled
geomorphic saddles, where
we, the heralds of freedom
would thus, fit the flash
suppressors of our
indiscriminate, automatic rifles
with unlubricated
latex covers, typically intended
as prophylaxis.

In the years that
would follow our war and my
subsequent isolation, I'd regret
having killed a jet-black
squirrel with my small
caliber farm rifle —
shot it off of the thornless
blackberry vines I'd grafted.
I'd also rue having wasted
a bounding brush rabbit
who'd chewed a hole
through the polypropylene
mesh of our apple orchard
— discovered it girdling
the base of one of the
young Gravensteins I'd
planted. And lest I forget,
sinking a beaver, intrinsically
acting-out in the meander
of autumn's noisy forest
stream — sank it out there
in the nocturne gnawing

alder and evergreen —
Out on the back forty
where it attempted to
flood our property.

But truth be told,
I never gave much thought
as to where those
ill-conceived rounds
would fall in the spring
and the summer of 1968
when I dropped a wealth
of those three pounders
down the steely throat
of a mortar tube,
not until I realized
the guilt that would
pursue me in the aftermath
of having been captive
to the eerie, inner sanctum
of imagery generated
by that far eastern
corner of my mind —

The haunting *mystère*
of those storied hills,
charred, hovering, and
all of them in stark contrast
to the sultry, lush abundance
of the jungled, variegated
valleys and kunai grass
below. It consumes me so

— the crackle and the
screams of burners engaging
as I continue to dream,
somnolent with the smells
and the sounds of
nightfall's napalm raining,
and the Bronx cheers
of the radio frequency noise
— those silver satanic angels
with their ravaging
Phantom strikes, to this
very day still strafe me,
deep into the stygian abyss
of my sleepless nights.

This is a past that goes
back better than half
a century now, and has taken
a sepia tone. And while
the jungles have prevailed
over all evidence of that war
— a war where I'd learned
that living muscle
would prove itself lighter
than that of the limp heft
of death—and that dose
of combat I'd imbibe,
would turn a docile lab rat
into an insidious pest
— a Jekyll and Hyde,
ever-reluctant to visit
with family and friends

— that my hideous side
might come out of hiding,
rear its ugly head
and ruin it for everybody.

I've heard from a few
down at the Legion Hall,
grappling over their
boiler makers and peanut pails
as to who'd won
and who hadn't.
What they wouldn't have
learned in the motor pools,
mess halls, and supply tents —

Battle and bloodshed
invariably yields no victors.

Fragmentations

Out of the Victorian
bay window Berkeley
and onto the Shattuck
Avenue approximation
to the defiant university,
subtitles literally spilt
from our mouths —
formed a lineage
of phonetics before us,
a visual syllabary
that danced from our lips,
the script to our secret
fraternal discourse.

And while we embraced,
my brother and I,
interwoven to
"Within You Without You,"
I held onto him for my life,
his wife, our babysitter,
glammed us with her
sitar rhythms, a score
with an aura of fuzz.
Outside, 'freaks and hairies'
roamed the earth.

Amid the contemporary
imperatives of American lit —
copies of r. crumb's

Mr. Natural, comic book God &
"Life Among the Constipated,"
juxtaposed to the
encyclopedic *I Ching*, and the
voluminous *Kama Sutra*
littering cold expansions
of hardwood, throw rug oak,
and the tremulous sprawl
of a raw-boned, nuclear holocaust cat,
the scrawny, naked lovers
may have called
Linoleum Water Heater

— when "Bear"
chemically engineered
500 grams of pure
"white lightning" in his
renaissance lab
of dichotomous, lysergic
labyrinthine frag men ta tions.

The Blue Cue

Down on Telegraph,
Angels congregated
— poised before their
chromium queues
of hogs aslant.
Motorcycle clubbers
quite capable of killing
— not cool cats
by any stretch, though
they'd all done stretches.
So you didn't give
these guys the stink eye,
man, these sentries
and sidekicks
to the Oakland kingpin,
Sonny Barger, back then
— black hearts strapped
with Lugers and switch-
blades held in hiding
on their unsunned, rubbed-
hairless legs — under the
aegis of their gamey,
black leather chaps.

These soldiers lined up shots
after breaking into
triangulated modifications
— racks for nine ball
cracking, blue chalk chalking,

squealing on the tips
of sticks miscuing.
Their grease monkey,
motor head mitts
rested on the cushions —
duct tape covering
the gouged attempts
at over-shaping
the two rail bank shots.

The worn leather lattice
of empty pockets refusing
to hold the strokes
of the sober and sloppy
drunk, some of whom,
in that savage crew,
preyed on fish — chum
like the toughs who'd
come in to play these mean,
badass, motherfuckers —
all of them monsters
and maestros of the *massé*
— homicidal, and pushers
of grade A junk.

They reeled this one kid in,
a diamond stud in his ear,
a face full of crude tattoos,

finally, had him on the line
for fifty bucks a game.
That was our old friend Roy —
took his Yamaha Street Scrambler
in full payment.

Leaving It to the "Beavers" of America

I wasn't crazy
nor was I queer
for Canada, not a pasty,
horn-rimmed,
preppie piss ant son
of a congressman.
I was hooked on
Lloyd Nolan and
Richard Conte —
on the Lieutenant
and the Sarge,
irrespective, ersatz
warriors, by and large.

And whilst we,
the television children
were paralyzed by
the patriotic,
Hollywood mantras —
those subliminal
clicking engagements
of fixed bayonets,
& in a likeness for the lotus,
sat glued; eyes rolled back
in our heads to a grainy,
black and white Motorola,
Tony Kubek autographed
baseball mitts in our laps.

We couldn't make
the distinction
in the comfort of our
Saturday afternoon
— colonial maple,
wall-to-wall low-pile
blue collar living rooms.
Rabbit ears askew
— snowy, hissing
credits running through
the finale of *Guadalcanal
Diary* — its soundtrack
the mellow, metallic,
to die for "Taps,"
hastening patriotic chills
up and down my spine,
ensued by the jingoistic,
tingling sensation
on the back of my
Cornish game hen neck,
the effects of which,
tracked the transmission
of a televised,
electromagnetically -
synthesized tenor
to a clandestine, DOD
movie studio laboratory.

Yes, I'd been
Twentieth Century
out-foxed by a film,
cited by the "NY Times"

as containing
"every cliché known to man"
all contrived in
a conspiracy to
brainwash the children
of America. My father
couldn't stop them.
He drove a Greyhound Bus
all day for a living.
Mother worked part-time
at Penny's, subjugated
herself to the old man
and his anger
— just as the gods
would have it. She too,
was unable to
deprogram me in the
purple haze of the Sixties.

My *nom de guerre*
would be Spunky,
an adrenalin junky, I'd
believe the lie. Later,
I'd pay my dues for mayhem
with mental illness.
Those who'd witness my
suffering may've asked me,
Why? O why, haven't you
put *this* all behind you?

And though I recognized
these vocal musings
as purely rhetorical, I would
simply offer that:
I am lost. Empty. Sick-sad,
with a dead excitement for life.
Nevermore would I explore
or fall prey to the sort of
palpable illusions like those
of a troubled drifter
in the *DSM's* shrunken
heads of text —
plumbing slumber's darkness,
bereft of those iconic days
gathering wool in Mayfield
ABC USA.

Beyond the Summer of Bummers and Love

Paraphrasing r. crumb,
"Everyone in the universe
is insane," making
perfect sense to me when
I was young and
living the lonely road,
tripping at the Fillmore
West to the Dead
Airplanes and Donovan
— love-ins at
Golden Gate Park. Hell,
I hopped freight trains
like I'd dreamed,
slumbered in the reeds
with guys just like me,
born to running from
the Fifties and convention.

But unbeknownst to the
sons of the quasi-fellaheen
back then, those of us who'd
volunteered, or were stunned
by conscription to serve
the carpet-bombing
architects — those absurd,
chicken-shit masterminds
and their specious recipes
for resolve, we'd be vilified
for the horrific verve

of the Tokyo and Osaka-like
B-29 blue prints they'd
indiscriminately use.

They'd chosen those of us
to arbitrarily don—
try on the camouflage veils,
involuntarily assail
a man whom we'd call
"Chan" to a masquerade
gala of tragic shadows.

Our struggles to recover
could not exceed
the ill effects of the guilt
we'd suffer, clearly
those debilitating periods
of combat fatigue — its
complement of unplumbed
hopeless desperation,
war-borne psychic lacerations,
and the very hairy swings
of hardcore *ennui*.

Home Sweet Hypocrisy

I came back home
a fucking catatonic
— back home
to the baked ham
and sour house shoe
Sunday Monday Tuesday
San Diego domicile,
where Greyhound was spoken
and socks were darned
— where rituals were practiced
and television worshiped.
And where I and the almighty
were drugged
and damned to hitchhike
into the concrete fisherman's
armpit plastered with pigeon shit
Frisco — inundated with the hip
deliberations that one might
devour, regurgitate,
and return to the road
— hop a freight train
to manic depression,
ever dispelling the myth
that blind faith prevails—
that this is a world of reason.

The City Snarled

The city snarled and bared its fangs
when I came out into the street
with my honorable discharge and my
purple fucking heart — to be wrestled
to the ground on the San Diego
downtown sidewalk concrete pavement
— choked-out by one of our finest,
a burly urban plainclothes porker.

Jesus Christ, I'd just come home
from Vietnam, muling in the tropics
for the fucking man, but nevertheless,
I'd spend the night on Avenue B,
all lit-up in a holding cell; rolling stale
tobacco with beat-up bums
and drunken skunks — just like me,
one summer eve, during Operation Intercept.

Man in the Window (Hillcrest 1969) for "The Fin"

The alarm
pierced my sleep. I woke.
And there
on the shelf that book I'd read.
I looked
out the window through my eyes
at all of those people —
urban throngs
of hungry thugs and greedy metro clones.
The razor
sliced my face. I bled.
And there in the tub that ball of hair.
I looked
out the window through my eyes
at all of those people —
those astir and frenzied
in a magnifying glass on a formicary.

I don't care,
when it's feet on feet
— when masses muster, then stampede.
The water
boiled. I took my tea.
And there on the wall that nude I'd sketched
I looked
out the window through my eyes
at all of those people —
junkies languished in their routine
chase for a fix through the city.

The comb
scratched my scalp. I shed.
And there on the floor that scale.
I looked
out the window through my eyes
at all of those people —
some for sale: a whore on a whore path
in lavender tights, squats to piss
in dawn's eroding, neon
alley's gumshoe strobe of lights.
The blue bus
came by and knocked them down. They broke.
And there in the street, cast like jacks,
an exhibit of bodies.
I looked
out the window through my eyes
at all of those people —

I couldn't quite see,
so I dropped another tab of LSD —
climbed aboard
an articulated serpent constricting,
rode the rage
of its wrenching slither,
o'er those muscular, tenderloin streets,
coursing on a bolt of "white lightning,"
the construct
of a clandestine chemist entrusted
with the malleable psyches
of our generation —
when I left my fickle ditz
of a girlfriend stranded, passed her off

on someone needier than I —
a crippled guy
who'd sat with me, hallucinating
and stupefied before Janis
and her entourage
of emaciated speed freak musicians,
their security, a motley queue —
Hell's Angelic crew of grisly henchmen.

Bouncing Around

I was quasi-seditious,
pandered myself
with an "Off the Pig" sign
for a ride through Soledad —
ate from the bags
of roaches and shake,
bouncing on a torn mattress
in the back of an old,
rusty panel truck, a
'51 Chevy stuffed
full of long hairs
& someone's mangy,
spaced-out, funky mutt
— pulled over
on the industry fringes
of Oakland and Berkeley,
hassled by the heat
just off the old Bay Bridge,
where the Zappa-like
freak at the wheel
could barely stay in his lane
for the wind.

Time would pass
& I'd catch a frosty ride
up through the sore throat
7AM (meth) amphetamine
state line. Semis grunted up
the white-knuckle grades

into the Siskiyou's
— wet snow sideways —
Shasta in the rearview mirror.

Up through Oregon and Washington
where eagles soared
over the sawmill emissions
and estuaries of Columbia's
gem of the industrial,
stinking ocean.

Up there where ravens and gulls
rummaged in the dumpsters
of the greasy off-road,
interstate dives,
where logging trucks, fog-fucked
into the Northwest
clear-cut, wildlife, wastelands.

The air still carried the fresh,
wet chill as I walked off
the Matanuska Ferry in Ketchikan
— May of Nineteen-seventy.

Between the Castle and Cannery Row

Moving north
along the pitted
California coastal byway,
en route to
the westernmost
hub of the revolution.
Snaking its blustery
sheer and terrible
beauty — doughty
in view of the might
in its potential
for unspeakable fate.
Sedated and
wending our way,
Nepenthean scoffing
at the palisades.
Serpentine winding
through the eerie brume,
where the evening's,
infinitely foamy,
black sea lathers
and licks at the skin
of the nebulous moon.

Faint in the misty
distance rising,
Kim Novak's asylum
from celebrity —
her stone and timber

octagon writhing
amid a flexing
throng of pine trees —
native anomalies
— exotic, stormy,
windswept deformities.
Uniquely Pacific;
specific to these
seaboard propagations of
contorted choreography,
where stage lights
fall upon the
iridescent waves — swells
that drub the crags
of the tidal shelves,
with energy enough
to summon the blubbers
of sea lions in their caves,
grottos beneath a garish
castle in the clouds
and above the imported
zebras grazing.

Indefatigable,
briny cymbals crashing,
pounding against the
barking, feral chambers
crowded — gasping
pockets of rock awash;
resounding, in what would
track a hundred miles
of hairpin curves, and

in the end display,
a placid evening's
radiant veil of embers
appearing to respire
on the lighted bluffs
above Monterey Bay.

Many Rivers to Remind Me

I lost count of the times,
thumbing up through the perils
and climes of the counter-cultured
coastline — Highway 1 of the
hippest times in our planet's history.
The zany zigzags abating
through Santa Cruz and San Fran,
warding-off with frequency
the random flashes in grim
retrospect — rekindled in the Coquille
entering the Pacific Ocean
at Bandon Dunes, the rocket
attacks and the contact
we'd made, operating
up on the Cửa Việt —
its suddenness of concussive,
hit-the-deck detonations —

Kabooms! triggered by the sour
chemistry and the ascension
of dark shoreline specters — tapered
smokestacks spewing ribs of toxic
gunmetal plumes across the Northwest
nimbostrati underbelly — mills belching
ghastly blooms that hover
the Willamette — white phosphorus-like
and doomsday wispy in the forested aeries
of cedar and fir —

Hueys chuff-chuffing..,
tremulous concentric ripples
on the surface of ponds
fetid in the open field's
rotor wash scramble,
sloshing through a maze
of dikes, immersed in the lecheries
of parasites leeching —
north of a trudge in our
buffalo mud-caked boots, where
a fire team from the 2nd platoon,
weighed down with the partial remains
of a kid on a blood-bathed
litter, tried to synchronize
their dissimilarity of lumbering gaits,
stuttered stumblings
that came back to me as I
likewise fumbled for my footing —

Up on the rainy day
railway tracks in Kelso,
on the daylight side of the 5 pm
still warm, gravel ballast,
and up from a camp
of hammered tramps — the Cowlitz,
like a tributary of the Perfume, roiling,
and where I watched the familiar
and the unfamiliar faces
of mortal men hoisted
onto a cargo floor, heard
that it was still slick with
the viscera of another mother's son

two hills over — one more LZ in Quang Tri
cut-out of the bamboo cordilleran
machete monkey jungle —

Guys around my age,
medevac'd out,
in the pre-dusk lift-off
— a limp arm dangling
from the cargo door —

Sitting on the roadside shaking
near Mount Vernon, no traffic freeway
exit/entrance, a barred owl posted
on a parliamentary fence aloft
the wavy-like razor grass bent —
gusty arcing — waiting hour
upon hour for a conservative
son of an immigrant Boer
to stoically offer me a ride
out of Amsterdam on the Skagit —
a lift to the border & out of the mouth
of another river's call to mind.

Enamored of the Art

I'd come to Alaska for asylum
and adventure. I couldn't
turn a blind eye
to the likeness I saw in myself
to that of Jack London,
— many ways akin
in our lack of naïveté,
both having witnessed
'the awful abysses of human
degradation' and decay,
yet hungered
for the spiritual richness
basic in bold,
wander lusting drifters.
I had a window seat
on the inside passage —
its soggy manifest
of pan-handle rain in buckets
curiously held a Klondike-like affect,
home of restless longings
— a white fang wealth of yearning
churning in my chest. Someone said,
"Loneliness is an art form"
and inasmuch as the pose
of a lone wolf's self-assured
silence, poised sublime
upon a precipice skyline,
I'd breathe deep —
complete my lungs with

Monet's air of rain-
forest mist, forged from
the quiet soggy, still life imagery
daubed from his raw, verdantly
variegated palette.

Sitka

We rode the borrowed
earth mover inner tubes,
glissaded down
the icy summer palomino
horsehide tunnels of
Harbor Mountain
— wheeled into town,
dried vomit in our beards,
wild and hairy
outside the Pioneer Bar
in the Indian Village.

Futile attempts at
eschewing the memory
of an old woman
I'd captured a world away,
beaten with a bandoleer
of seven six twos,
I'd fail to revive my ethos
— my poor soul, sore
with loneliness
and craving females
for drunken fornication.
Yet, in lieu, I'd pass out
in the mossy rotted
boardwalk, fishgut drizzle.

Jamming With Dead Russians

In my Romeo's and long johns,
I pissed from the elevated
treehouse veranda — a drunken elf,
golden arcing from 30 feet above
& onto a Russian cemetery.

We'd have sessions up there
with fishery bums, slime line workers,
and a motley of cannery slaves,
slaving down at the cold storage
quay on Conway Dock.

Wild children and hairy vagabonds
biked down — leaned their rides
against the crustose lichen-obscured,
surnamed grave markers
of Petrov and Mishkin.

I played in an ensemble
with my homemade instrument:
mop handle, clothesline,
and a metal wash basin. Cold drafts
often rose to the occasion.

In Town They Called Our Craft
a Creek-Robbing Scow

At the helm, a vodka-guzzling,
local native salt & seal skinner,
and cooking, his cousin — a man
who'd barely survived
a village fire. He wore a melted mask
for a face. They shared
the indigenous affliction
of cirrhotic livers, perpetually
processing spirits — night upon night,
anchored and buoyant
in the cabin's candlelight swollen with flies.

Topside one night and bobbing about,
our fucked-up skipper
blew a hole through one of the floor-
board planks. Below deck
and cackling on our cots, something
was just so damned funny —
we were smoking pot
when that sobering, misfired slug,
just missed my good friend, Dickie.

And for that mere trifle, we gave thanks
to the powers that be.
So, with the nebulous sun
in the six o'clock sky,
we collected our earnings
or ran from our debt.

I returned to the muskeg, skunk cabbage,
and fiddleheads — back to my
devil's club, nightclubs,
and graveyard treehouse
— to my sketchy recitals
at the Potlatch House,
where gnarly, encrusted loggers,
thick as Sitka Spruce;
Angoon Pete and Hog Legs,
Moss, J.D., and Moose
— flannel fuckers all, swilling tubs of beer,
laughed above my lyrics,
sniffed my verse for fear.

Dickie would move on to the potato fields
of Madras.

Martha

It was 1970 & I was
far away in an evergreen dream,
playing bass fiddle washtub
alongside two guys
who'd hitched-up with me
from San Mateo.
Accompanied by guitars,
harmonicas, and mutts, we
hired-on as deckhands —
piling cork and mending seine,
preying on the wild,
lonely passions of the cannery
women in Chatham.

I met a young woman
from Bellingham —
her scent my addiction.
The damp silk curls
of her hippie brunette armpits,
her magic French kiss,
northwest fair skin complexion
fueled my excitement,
embroiled on a bank southwest
of Hoonah, where mosquitoes
feasted on our bare flesh,
shared our psilocybin
delirium of chicken wire
and dragons on the sky.

Lumbering brown bears
left their etchings in the timber
and their scat in the sand.
The day before, we'd boiled crabs
that I'd stolen from the Filipinos
— they would've killed me.

Mending Seine

I

One of two white men aboard,
I turned my head to hide my laughter
amid the rubber tongue
toothless slaver of the native seiners
— articulations, utterly awash
in a swamp of hyper-salivation,
and further waxed by the wads
of the chaw they chewed.
Their mother tongue already molested
by the fur trade invaders
and missionaries who
imported the fricative and the alveolar
of Cyrillic sound — a compound
of Orthodox Russian
and the rattling croak
from the gargling throat
of a raven — deliberations as to
where the humpbacks might blow next,
a mountainous wet
of geyser–like spewing
off the face of the jellyfish sea.

Our nascent crew of native sons
and long hairs — dark arms
etched with a tribal gradient of tattoos —
symbols from the discerning
to the diminished, ubiquitous displays
of blue-black wing span spirits,
inked totemic

on the appendages of both
young and old Tlingits. I wish
I could remember
their Christian names, those
who'd place their bets
as to whether,
the shattering breach of some
mythical, ivory giant
might bring ruin — devour
our entire fleet like krill,
doing sets outside of Tenakee.

        II

Across that windswept span of bay,
bald eagles appeared to claim
exclusive rights to the tops of trees.
A myriad of white crops
dotting the Sitka spruce,
and a hemlock sweep
of panhandle coastline.
Its quintessential vision kissed
on a gray slate bias of July mist.
It was there, an erstwhile,
distant cannery vanished
in the inverted grip of a somber clime,
and wherein, sheer cliffs hovered
before creosote quays, that had
likewise passed from our sight,
along with an anchored, offshore tender.
Its crew of Japanese hurled a detritus
of Pinks on the bight and,
into the screeching din of herring gulls,

sharing a wealth of bycatch
with a host of pelagic nomads
against the wail of the wind
and the same current carrying
the smoldering scent of charred ruins
— a trapper's cabin, remote and
sheltered in a quiet cove;
an abandoned pot belly stove
matching the shade of a lone black bear
salvaging in the solace of ribs
on the tide.

III

Our skipper slurred and listed,
pendulous upon his
teetering perch, failed to conceal
the frequent pulls he took
from a Wódka bottle, all too obvious
in the marsupial green sac
of a sea suit reeling with hubris
and a Remington. His besotted,
bloodshot eyeball, vertiginous
in the crosshairs, but nonetheless,
trained on a harbor seal fucking
with the fathoms of salmon distended seine.

IV

Blustery blasted, windy drenching,
cold in the downpour skiff,
I sat idling in the rain — shivering,
rubber-hooded, bumping-up against
the bobbing, wind-felled corpse

of an evergreen.
Dreaming out there on the briny
of my paltry share of the take —
choking on the vapors from the gasoline,
just inside the break, a black tail
(a doe methinks), half-galloped frantic
— a reflex to our underbelly's
seeping escapement.
Its obscene, swirling sheen
perverted the wake,
washing over the conspicuous tic
on her pristine hide, head-high
on the choppy, and just astride
the buoyant, encrusted façade
of our nodding scow.

              V

The vessel's shedding, flaking dedication
in Gothic font, appeared painted
on the port of her weathered prow.
But unlike the name
of our seafaring vessel,
and the Christian names
that have escaped my failing mind,
respectively drubbed with salinity
and the steel wool
of passing time, I haven't been able
to dispense with the squealing strain
from the deck of our
power block hoisting those bloated
monster sets, brimming with a frenzy
of fins and gills constrained

— nor of the ocean spilling with profusion,
rising out of those cold Alaskan depths,
where there were sea nettle crowns
for the Kings and Reds,
energized in a marinade of yellow kelp
and glacial silt — a translucent
hysteria of glass-eyed heads immersed
and very much alive,
save for the flux of the cadaverous fish,
a surge of silken milky corpses
astride a churn of sediments rich
with ocean and naked earth —
its unrivaled redolence steeped
in the stubborn, sinewy mesh
of this native seiner's purse.

Pride of the Sound

We slept into the nights
of the foggy chimes
and in those dreams
on the ocean's sway,
awoke on the break
of the sun and a new day
which hastened our crew
to thirty-two hours,
in a timeless pursuit
amid the power block showers
— where I'd bend at the crest
of those blue taut waves.

By me, my God
this quest I'd sought
at edges end — to send me
to the sound
and airless ocean floor. I'd
beg to see *thee* soggy pit,
wander explosive and
bloated across *thy* salty,
silted bed.

I carried a bottle
of Lord Calvert's
in my sea suit.
"Three sheets to the wind,"
I'd howl for the fish
that fought, slurred,

"Damn Rights"
when stubborn Sockeyes
gnawed through our nets.

Sick from the whiskey
and the list of this
lapping lilt, I did
brashly heave into the
drone of wounded
carburetor and the slimy
sauce of the sea that spilt.

From stern to bow
ten times a day, we'd pitch
our scaly, hapless,
captives away
into the stinking hold
of the boat, and wherewith,
(our) buckets of saltwater,
we'd wash the decks
of the Coho and the King —

Slimy slicks with
briny bits of yellow kelp
and the red sea nettle
crowns of the jellyfish
— tentacles that
rained from the lazy
drapes of nylon seine.
Its generosity o' stingers
stung with the hot,
toxic saliva

from a sea demons' tongue,
better known to these parts
as Lion's Mane
— rusty tangles snarling
in the wakes of Sitka Sound.

Family Doctor

Dr. Francis injected me
with an antigen,
a toxoid that would
prevent me from
contracting lockjaw,
having bailed, as a child
from a plywood shack —
haphazardly tacked
into a stand of eucalypti.
I landed on a plank
with a rusty ten penny
— spike face up, into my
tennis shoe foot.

Years later, our doctor's son
would attain the rank of
captain in the Green Berets
— would come by the status
of KIA, dying in the jungle
below a hill crawling with
a weathered, leatherneck
lot — my grungy, amoral
rifle company and a
regiment of rats in '68.

I was staying with an old
girlfriend a year or so after
the war, when I became
very ill with a visiting virus.

My mother came over to
collect me, took me to see
old Doc Francis.

Unshaven, encrusted,
pissed at the world
for all of the obvious reasons,
I hadn't been keeping good
hygiene, and he couldn't
disguise his disgust for a child
he'd treated with a tetanus
shot, those erstwhile, nebulous
'salad days' in fact,
he scolded me
with a cancer in his heart,
as two years prior & still
in shock, *his* progeny had
returned from the jungle
in a flag-draped box.

Black's Beach, Pacific Ocean

A hundred seals
barked and blubbered
— their inner tube hides
donned muted sheens.
A hundred seals
on ocean boulders,
wailed in a wake
of swollen foam
— swells that slammed
the jetty shoulders,
mopped with generous
coats of creosote.

Sitting in a mist
of flies in fleets,
nourishing in the tangled
wreckage of mussels,
a cormorant's quill,
and the luster of
amber sheets
in a strangle of kelp,
where the breeze
kissed my cheeks —

Its wealth of gusty busses
blew in on a stiff, off-
shore trade wind of lips,
where breakers born
of the trembling earth,

concurrently dowse
and drench with furls of foam
the sunbaked and saline
crown of a sandstone
bluff bejeweled
with the barnacles
of acorn acne,
afore a colony of gulls
in a sea of squalls
like laughter — they'd
slather those scarps
with a primer
of feculent plaster.

The shelves on the cliffs
of La Jolla — a palette
of palisades towering
above a hundred seals
— bouncing like my
liberated female friends
who'd eventually follow
my fading foot prints
into the head-on, whitecap
bluster of the Pacific Ocean.

Bakersfield to Fresno

I caught the rusty grip
on that last car's
generational freight train buggy,
along with a nose full
of diesel belches —
air-borne additions
to the pesticide emissions
— Kern County's
poisonous mists & not to mention,
so why mention,
the creosote blisters
under the dry Central Valley sky,
bloated & bubbling
on railroad ties where I bailed
on the fly, tore one of my
palms open — rupturing
an expansive vesicle I'd acquired
having erstwhile,
rested my hand on an exhaust pipe
three days prior
in 71's heat of the noonday sun,
and in so splaying,
a vagabond's version of the
Superman sprawl,
out and across the railway ballast,
I crawled away from the subgrade
of gravel skirting the tracks,
when I discovered I'd broken the strap
to that little ruck upon my back.

The Mill

The dog I'd been feeding had a girlfriend,
I called Noodles. They'd carry on, wandered
about town with a certain amusing alacrity
while my days were spent laboring in the
chemical stench of a pulp mill 5 miles east
of Sitka. Owned by the Japanese, and
employing a goodly number of mostly men
supporting families, I was hired for the summer,
owing to the generosity of the veteran
mill nurse out there — wife of the Episcopalian
priest at St. Peters by the Sea. I'd groomed
their son, a boy 14, to play the part of my
younger brother, when she decided to exert
her influence on my behalf, having sewn-up
enough on-site relationships out there, to pull some
sutures for me.

My days that summer were spent severing
the metal bands cinching bundles of pressure-
wrapped Western Hemlock and Sitka Spruce,
hoisted up and slurping with red toxic jelly
and enough squeaky brown, bull kelp, to slap you silly —
onto a deck 60 feet above the log pond, a peril that
inarguably required I wear a forestry safety helmet
and visor, stand behind an iron shield and wield
one of those heavy duty, industrial strap cutters **SNAP!**
A thunder-clap of massive timbers exploded —
rolled like an avalanche of tumbling boulders up there,
turned, debarked, and pulverized into
pulp for rayon and paper.

Or, I may have drawn the task requiring me
to be steeped into an (empty) tank, lowered in
with another yard slave, often this Filipino who'd
been hired on at inception. The things we'd carry:
a tin of Copenhagen, drop light, mallet, and a chisel
for chipping away at the stubborn, baked-on, red
liquor deposits, cemented to the vessel's interior walls.

Or, I may have been above the smoke-billowing,
steamy, stinky silo-like structures towering above
that complex, walking the beltline ramps, shoveling
the conveyor spillage of sawdust, hiding in a dark
corner from the foreman, and killing time until the whistle
sounded for lunch or shift change at 3. I was saving
for a trip back to the Far East, mindful of the debauchery,
and the myriad opiated options, available to me.

My ride and I would stop at the Three and a Half for a beer
and a look-see at the tattooed dancers after work and I told
this guy, Mike, I think (it's been 50 years) I had to feed
my dog and I knew I could always find those two animals
in tandem pleading for treats in the alley behind the Sitka
Café, or on Lincoln St. where tendered tourists browsed
store fronts across from the Pioneer Home.

Hot Springs

Coniferous corpses
impaled on the low tide
two coves south
of comic puffins,
performing standup
on mussel-crusty cliffs
— did their shticks
for an audience
of murres, petrels, and
otters lounging
on couches of kelp.

Tom and I and Blue
powered into another
bay floating with
common eiders and
canvasbacks. Taking
the marsh land trail,
one of them,
wary of bear, toted
a thirty aught six.

We'd come to this place
to soak in a state
of geothermal satori.
In Goddard, simmering
springs would boil you
light-headed — pure silence
crisping on the air, a distal

idiomatic undercurrent of
encrypted words —
mantras seeping out
from the soft sponge of earth.

On the Bum in '72

I'm a Scottish-Irish,
Hungarian-Cherokee,
Polack-Jew,
who went off to war,
back in the day
when they weren't
calling us heroes
anymore. In fact,
I heard they
spat on me
but I didn't go to
Vietnam for Uncle Sam.
I, like every other
young fuck — we
sorry young bucks
back then,
wanted to emulate
our uncles in Korea,
or in some other
Cinemascopic,
technicolored,
amphibious assault
on some other
paradisiacal paradox
of a beachhead,
only this time
headlining yours truly –
freckled acquaintance
to the gonzo journalist,

friend slash nemesis
of Lou Reed. *Me*, who
took a Greyhound Bus
through the Bible Belt
and into the barbequed
steakhouse hunting dog,
Republican crew cab
evangelical snakebite
Christianity. *Me*,
on my way back
from Thailand, still
groggy from the narcotics,
Uh huh, crewcut pickup
gun rack — and those
old boys had a real case
of the ass. Their women
sported 1955 cotton candy
hairdos. *Me*, glad to finally
get back at my *escritoire* —
anxious for my art to free up
so I could write about
something other than my pain.
Me, who hopped
an eastbound in January,
keeping to myself
the ghastly odor
of weeks unwashed,
zipped-up and shivering
in my mummy bag —
the bounce and the growl
in my spine — high desert
Reno to Salt Lake

– 500 mile frozen
midnight boxcar bedlam,
and the tracks whizzed by
and the Kerouac
within *me* cried
'cuz *me* had a certain
bonhomie with alcoholic poets,
vogues and bums.

Anticipating a Job in the Valley

The thick,
acrid air of perspiration
and flatulence
permeated the scenic cruiser
as it departed El Centro for
Tucson.

A four hundred pound
female Cocopah
labored up the aisle
and took two seats.
The driver tightened his grip
on the wheel
as the large woman displayed
a grand smile —
the hues of Indian corn.

Chatty *braceros*,
machine gun tongues
on full automatic,
shot the breeze with respect
to the hard work
and lean wages, while
cervezas baratas
were discreetly passed around.

There was a thin brown man
in every seat. Each one
appeared to sport

un sombrero de vaquero,
hecho de jipijapa.
All donned stiff Levis,
white long sleeves,
and dusty worn western,
leather boots - no belt.

One of the migrant workers
with a poker face said,
the bus he'd ridden last season,
damn-near tipped-over
after a collision with
a large tarantula crossing the road.
The spider eventually caved
under the weight of the bus,
but not before
much concern was given.

All in earshot
gave pause momentarily
at the laughably, inane image
of eight legs lumbering
out of a blind wash on Old Hwy 80
— suddenly breaking
into an outburst of mass hysteria.

Tarantula gigante!
one of them wailed and held his side.

These *muchachos*
would begin their treks this night, bedrolls
slung over their shoulders

— back across into *Mexico*,
through the barbed wire and searchlights.
They'd bed down on the floor
of the Sonoran Desert
with the jack rabbits and ground owls,
rattlesnakes and scorpions.
Tomorrow, *por la tarde*,
they would be home with their families
in *Tajitos*, and the towns
and villages scattered along
the *Arroyo El Coyote*.

Under a Bridge in the Pouring Rain

Unable to acquire
a prosthetic psyche
in Seventy-two, my
pathetic character
came unglued
and I ramped-up
my tolerance
for goofballs and booze.

I found supplication
and self-medication,
ephemeral solutions
to my psychic pain,
while lending my ears
to the illusively unending,
hissing of cars all day.

Under a bridge in the
pouring rain, I'd
sit on a plywood sheet
I'd scrounged, and
shake. All lit-up,
or a' glaze in a stupor,
I'd vegetate to the hush
and the whisper
of wet revolutions.

Up on the interstate
the scent of

petrichor and rubber,
a fragrance, not
inconsistent with that
of the gusty, precipitous
highland climes —
Indochinese,
tropical monsoon downpour
biases, for and against
its sheer terrain

— of the *theia mania*
and the Tiger Whiskey
to kill my pain
like Ares who had
married his words
with Olympian wine
— elocutions
entirely analogous
to the after effects
of those myriad
chemicals I'd ingest
— those owing to my
petitions before
a heavenly father.
Hadn't his madness
seemed simply divine?

High Desert

Freight cars rattled
the Flagstaff night,
shook through a neon
cross-country mecca
of train yard souls.

A Motel 6 at 3 a.m.
— elastic silhouettes
spanned the peel
and the cracks of
paint and plaster.

Rheumy-eyed and
rolling smokes, doing
solo shots into
the dawn's eroding,
spastic strobe.

Glowing embers ebbed
and flowed on the pulse
of a bursting mescal
blood-orange sunrise,
& a poet's cry was realized,

Out on the stitched-up
illusions of the radiant
open road's black top
heat wave oases, where
users go to score a fix

Out on the double-line,
speed-bumping,
serpentine, Rte. 66
sutures. Strung-out
and sidewinding

The 17 South to Sedona
— Oak Creek to Phoenix,
and out of its finite fire
of tumbleweed undulations.
Tied-off & spiked to the vista's

Canvas with a coral blush,
where saguaros
and train tracks stagger,
along the golden arms
of dusk.

Stargazing

Tattered tramps
nestled in the sage.
Their spirits
numbed by frostbite,
arthritis,
and the profound,
bloody-knuckle,
nose-drip-sizzle
of a still life
manzanita blaze.

A four in the morning
fire pumped
black plumes high
into the apprehensive
cold steel
and wooden underbelly
of a trestle trembling,
in the pre-dawn,
stellar castings
on a winter arroyo.

A freight train slowed
at the bend in the river.
Screeching brakes,
scraped the spines
of hobos braced
for another day
of desert sunshine

— where frost
would leech from loins,
and testicles
retract in groins
— lest they'd be crushed
by a shifting load.
Those gnarly nomads
with ascending gonads,
a fire pit diffused
by a gravel road.

And ere the trade
of flames for smolder,
one of their bulging,
besotted-eyeballs
scanned,
a desert crest
of granite boulders,
in awe of that barren,
pre-dawn land.

Its shivering litany
of yips and yowls,
a lonesome,
chilling lilt that swept
the sweep of dunes,
assuaged by the mating call
of a horned owl
growling at silhouettes
framed on the face
of a vanishing moon.

Still, enough of a moon
to shed some light,
casting shadows
on the final pulls
of Bali Hai, and of those
freeloaders on those
flat cars, with the reedy
renderings of mouth harps
whined —

Woody Guthrie tunes
that would play ensemble
with the defrosted
whimpering of coyote cries,
& the screech & squeal
of ferrous wheels —
smoking cigars,
watching stars diminish
into the morning sky.

Sundown Jungle Texarkana

In stranded boxcars,
just up from the
perennial tangerine harvests
of Southern Florida, tramps
like mummies, coiled
in corners, slumbered
on the rife with chink
and the splintered
slats of the yellow pine
knot holes. Two days prior
and proffering, the nomad
prostrate, gravel spyglass
offerings — those obtuse
freight car views, figure
eight-like serpentine skewed
and wending on better
than a zephyr witness.
The unshaven rye whiskey
and fellaheen wander-lusting
kings of the railroad krazy —
liberated souls all
liquored-up and holy-toed,
nearby a lazy stone brook
mewling, loitering alongside
a white oak bivouac campsite
stagger — where a wild, drunken
clutch of bloody knuckles
struck a tree, an errant,
fractured fist of a roundhouse

punch thrown, just wide of its
mop-headed target,
a tattooed loner outta
Tennessee, who done
brought an innuendo
to a soliloquy:
(*Some folk just don't take kindly
to thieves*)
Another barefoot, freight-
jump'n fool, a chucklehead
glued to his seat — there on
a stump-like stool of oak,
bleat'n and a' chok'n on a
throat full of juice, a mixture
distilled from a wad of Red Man
chew and a swig of Kentucky
bourbon. His worn boots swung
intolerant to the leeching aloft
the hobo stewpot jungle fire,
while possums was skewered
& frogs was gigged & slow dripped
flicker'n — into the spit of the
fat slop popp'n, like shoe rags
to the toothless gumm'n.
Mouth harps humm'n "Dixie"
— piercing the night with its cadence
of wounded fifer's limping
tympanic with vacillations
of the drumsticks' hickory,
— into the evening's cricketing
moonlight countryside, where
the waves of the grassy midnight

badlands, bent a full head
of golden hair in the howling
of wind shears — out there
on the divides of stage lights
filtering an array of stars
that shone on the devils of dust
portending. Its babble
of mystical tongues, lapping
at the sun-dropped death
of lighted day.

Tribute to the Dead Beats

> "...creating a spontaneous bop prosody..."
> — Allen Ginsberg

If I were obliged to aspire
to the works of Rod McKuen,
the world as I have known it,
would, with combustible
spontaneity, set itself afire,
smolder into the black hole dusk
and extinguish on the cusp
of utter ruin.

Instead, I gave my allegiance
to the ugly, bearded, beatnik Jew
— the squalid, Howling maniac,
50s and 60s Paterson pal
to the incurably, krazy Kerouac.
I opted to fill my lungs with skunk
in an alley. Live my days
in a briny haze, of murky piers
and fish gut galleys. Yes,
I went that-a-way,
with the "Slobs of the Kitchen Sea"
hopped freight trains and slept
in jungles; survived *On the Road*
with the 'King of the Beats'

Astir in a (con) fusion as to who
we were back then, beginning to
and/or begotten by the end

of a sort of an ascetic, Gary Snyder-
like, transcendent of the Beat,
Buddhistic hippie. The old brotherhood
like the new brotherhood, lost
or found themselves in a velvet
underground of rock and roll,
narcotic psychoses
— peace piping cadres who'd take hits
of the craze, fringing on the peyote
nation, or they'd tie-off & fix
— share needles and chicks,
staggering along those gateway miles
to the urban vials of tenement smack.

Portland's junkies like my brother's
friends, Houghton and Babcock —
with their soot tattoos, mainline trains
on ebon tracks; hard core hep cats,
shooting-up and ventilating to the
jazz masters of the cosmic, musical zoo
— while all the while,
I was just passing through.

Wood Smoke Tracking the Tanana

Evening skies that week
had worn the tufts, sunsets awash
on nigh to nightfall's breasts
of rosella. October's pre-dusk
first snow, like feathers fell —
drowsy flakes of down adrift
on lazy breezes circling a desolate
hinterland dwelling, eighty years
a construct before McKinley's
southern face — a trapper's cabin
sown unto a tundra glade.
Its somber aura weighed on the cold,
distant fringes of still isolation.
Billows curled from its smokestack —
a black iron tube, poking through
the green sod roof, plumes leveling-
out on hibernal fledgling currents
blowing in off the gelid flush of
Wrangell Mts. tribute to the Yukon River.

Really Big Fucking Hands and Feet

Waiting for me and our
weekly games of crib,
my gnarly neighbor
wrung the icicles
from his crop of
wild ginger follicles,
then tweezed slivers
of black spruce piercing
his dry, fissured hands
from the freezing weather.

Upon forcing the ice-bound
door, trappings of what
I saw, a catalog —
of leather gloves, big enough
to fit a brown bear's paw,
a cup of joe like mud
atop a potbelly stove,
and after miles of
trekking deep marshland
snow, the jumbo set
of wicker walkers I'd been
tracking.

It was in that moment
my eyes picked up
the wet crescent launch

— a spent wad of snuff
splashing down into a
wonted week-old sea
of spittle. The reservoir,
a rusty Hills Bros tin
abutting a bottle of Jameson's.

Hunting Trip

On a mountain above Starrigavan Creek,
we gutted and drug — carried-out about
two hundred pounds of quartered
black tail meat, stumbling amid fiddleheads,
fireweed and forget-me-nots, where we drew
a ravenous cloud of flesh flies hunting a home
to hide their roil of maggots.

Bears outnumbered humans up there —
evidenced by the myriad ursine tracks
of blueberry scat and where I'd find myself
very serious in the all-day Baranof Island sun,
batting at swarms of white sox with one
free arm, side-stepping a waddling porcupine
(the first I'd seen) but foremost, wary
with 'bearanoia' — a crude cloven haunch
upon my shoulder.

In the Zen of the River

I'd come into town
from the woods for my
weekly protein fix,
a four course at the
Sitka Café, after which,
I'd wander out and
watch the crabs
sideways dancing
in the jags of basalt
and beneath the bridge
that brought the jobs
and the carbon emissions
to Mount Edgecumbe.

I lived on a diet of
brown rice, fiddleheads, and
smoked salmon — when
the rains came and washed
my campsite down the river
and into the sea,
during the summer of '73
— washed me out of the woods
where my treehouse stood,
a structure from whence
I'd continuously target
the confounding *ennui,*
and the flashbacks
that I'd lived with, nigh
two miles into the Tongass,

where I would typically
be found tripping around
on LSD or soused on a hue
of tangerine fluid
I'd kept in an exhausted
two liter bottle of James Dean.

It was around that time
I was shanghaied by a
redheaded woman, stolen
into her heart and made
to explain my situation
before she'd accept
a wild hairy beast from the forest
into her house. Still very
much stuck in the mire
of convention, my dire psyche
betrothed on the stake
to a beating of solitude,
and the countless lashes
in the lingering aftermath
of blues postbellum —
haunting my adventures
in that period of jazz cigarettes
and psychedelia —

Its eerie drear of coming-on-to,
and peaking in the all-nighters
— babysitters like
designated drivers who'd
get us through those changes
of mental agony, and where I

discovered myself hiding
from everything that reminded me
of my time, in what the Vietnamese
would call, 'The American War,'
and how similarly, this redheaded
woman I'd met, escaped L. A.
on a Xmas eve flight to Alaska
— fleeing a contentious divorce
with her baby.

And thus, came the pots and the pans,
reserves of the rubbish I'd amassed
— liberated vestiges on the squalling
throngs of inclement weather.
And as the clouds of cognitive disorder,
blew out on this storm of passion
— so did the interminable hours
we'd spend in a dizzy,
sensual zen of carnal kissing —
its impetus released
on the passing of this panhandle
tempest — leaving us to our
passions on a dry, wind-felled
giant above Indian River —
inflexibly spanning the shore-
to-shore gargle of swollen fury.

Still Smoldering After All These Years

There's nothing like a good reminder
of the artillery I was so fond of
from my days 'in country'
Pirate ships on the harbor
reenact historical high seas conflicts
with cannon blasts —
simulated, Sixteenth Century duels
waged, here in San Diego
where I live in a condominium
with my lover.
More than fifty years have elapsed
since I saw action in Southeast Asia,
yet those booms on the bay
never fail to kick my ass,
and thus, perpetuate my wont to rage.

I was quietly recounting one thing
or another, the other day,
when my wife yanked at a Velcro strap
attached to the geriatric apparatus
supporting her ancient leg
— a noise that, prior to impact,
was entirely reminiscent
of the sheer trajectory and caterwauling
crescendo of an incoming eighty-deuce.
With an eerie prescience,
one of the galleons,
just shy of simultaneous,
fired two of its four faux guns.

And I asked myself in that apropos
moment of recovery—

How many years more will the embers of war
smolder as such, inside me.

About the Author

Fred Rosenblum grew up in SoCal during the 50s – 60s, a blue-collar kid and one of the "television children fed," via a Motorola, a smorgasbord of baloney and American cheese. And while Fred's father was a bus driver and a Freemason, and his mother held a station in the Eastern Star at the Chula Vista chapter — they'd see it all in black and white ... until, February of 1968, when color seemed affordable, and real blood became red. Without the Cronkite narrative, Vietnam presented their nineteen year old with an eyewitness account of the TET Offensive — acting as security for a convoy running supplies into the ruins of Hue City. The ensuing 13 month stretch spent 'humping' the mountainous jungled terrain of the RVN's I Corps sector would impact Fred and his present and future family's lives on this planet like no other event, historical or otherwise. It would color his every endeavor, in the workplace and in the hearth. The struggle to forget never ends, but with time, harsh realities tend to wither somewhat. Moreover, and arguably cathartic, four books of poetry have been gleaned from this struggle. In 2011, following a 36 year odyssey in Alaska and the Northwest, Fred returned to his hometown of San Diego, CA with his wife and muse of too many years, where they now enjoy a very therapeutic existence 'in the warm California Sun.'

Fomite

More poetry from Fomite...
Anna Blackmer — *Hexagrams*
L. Brown — *Loopholes*
Sue D. Burton — *Little Steel*
Christine Butterworth-McDermott — *Evelyn As*
David Cavanagh— *Cycling in Plato's Cave*
James Connolly — *Picking Up the Bodies*
Greg Delanty — *Loosestrife*
Mason Drukman — *Drawing on Life*
J. C. Ellefson — *Foreign Tales of Exemplum and Woe*
Tina Escaja/Mark Eisner — *Caida Libre/Free Fall*
Anna Faktorovich — *Improvisational Arguments*
Barry Goldensohn — *Snake in the Spine, Wolf in the Heart*
Barry Goldensohn — *The Hundred Yard Dash Man*
Barry Goldensohn — *The Listener Aspires to the Condition of Music*
Barry Goldensohn — *Visitors Entrance*
R. L. Green — *When You Remember Deir Yassin*
KJ Hannah Greenberg — *Beast There—Don't That*
Gail Holst-Warhaft — *Lucky Country*
Judith Kerman — *Definitions*
Joseph Lamport — *Enlightenment*
Raymond Luczak — *A Babble of Objects*
Kate Magill — *Roadworthy Creature, Roadworthy Craft*
Tony Magistrale — *Entanglements*
Gary Mesick — *General Discharge*
Giorigio Mobili — *Sunken Boulevards*
Andreas Nolte — *Mascha: The Poems of Mascha Kaléko*
Sherry Olson — *Four-Way Stop*
Brett Ortler — *Lessons of the Dead*
David Polk — *Drinking the River*
Janice Miller Potter — *Meanwell*
Janice Miller Potter — *Thoreau's Umbrella*
Philip Ramp — *The Melancholy of a Life as the Joy of Living It Slowly Chills*
Joseph D. Reich — *A Case Study of Werewolves*
Joseph D. Reich — *Connecting the Dots to Shangrila*
Joseph D. Reich — *The Derivation of Cowboys and Indians*
Joseph D. Reich — *The Hole That Runs Through Utopia*
Joseph D. Reich — *The Housing Market*
Kenneth Rosen and Richard Wilson — *Gomorrah*
Fred Rosenblum — *Playing Chicken with an Iron Horse*
Fred Rosenblum — *Tramping Solo*
Fred Rosenblum — *Vietnumb *
David Schein — *My Murder and Other Local News*
Harold Schweizer — *Miriam's Book*
Scott T. Starbuck — *Carbonfish Blues*

Fomite

Scott T. Starbuck — *Hawk on Wire*
Scott T. Starbuck — *Industrial Oz*
Seth Steinzor — *Among the Lost*
Seth Steinzor — *Once Was Lost*
Seth Steinzor — *To Join the Lost*
Susan Thomas — *In the Sadness Museum*
Susan Thomas — *The Empty Notebook Interrogates Itself*
Sharon Webster — *Everyone Lives Here*
Tony Whedon — *The Tres Riches Heures*
Tony Whedon — *The Falkland Quartet*
Claire Zoghb — *Dispatches from Everest*

Dual Language
Vito Bonito/Alison Grimaldi Donahue — *Soffiata Via/Blown Away*
Antonello Borra/Blossom Kirschenbaum — *Alfabestiario*
Antonello Borra/Blossom Kirschenbaum — *AlphaBetaBestiaro*
Antonello Borra/Anis Memon — *Fabbrica delle idee/The Factory of Ideas*
Aristea Papalexandrou/Philip Ramp — *Μας προσπερνά/It's Overtaking Us*
Katerina Anghelaki-Rooke//Philip Ramp — *Losing Appetite for Existence*
Jeannette Clariond/Lawrence Schimel — *Desert Memory*
Mikis Theodoraksi/Gail Holst-Warhaft — *The House with the Scorpions*
Paolo Valesio/Todd Portnowitz — *La Mezzanotte di Spoleto/Midnight in Spoleto*

Writing a review on social media sites for readers will help the progress of independent publishing. To submit a review, go to the book page on any of the sites and follow the links for reviews. Books from independent presses rely on reader-to-reader communications.

For more information or to order any of our books, visit:
http://www.fomitepress.com/our-books.html

www.ingramcontent.com/pod-product-compliance
Lightning Source LLC
Chambersburg PA
CBHW021429070526
44577CB00001B/125